THE EXCELLENCE BOOK

104 Principles for Living and Working

WRITTEN BY

Dana LaMon

PUBLISHED BY

2000

ISBN: 0-9656633-4-5

Library of Congress   Catalog   Number:
00-132466

ImageWorth

Post Office Box 6108
Lancaster, California 93539-6108
(661) 949-7423

Printed in the United States of America

First ImageWorth Printing: June 2000.
Second ImageWorth Printing: June 2007.

Raphael Villar Jr.
108 Larkspur Dr.
Salinas, CA 93906-3805

DEDICATION

TO
JACQUELINE
DANA and WINTER
ANTON and LINNEA

May 20, 2000

Dear Reader,

I am stuck on excellence. I got stuck as I contemplated my life, my job, and my career and considered what my focus should be in the new millennium. Repeatedly the word excellence flashed in my head.

On the first day of the year 2000 I wrote several principles of excellence. The next day I wrote more. I did not know where the writing would lead until I began sharing the principles with friends and clients, and they asked for copies of them.

I present here 104 principles of excellence. They are not just principles for working but also for living. Why 104? Well, that's where I got stuck.

Dana LaMon
Lancaster, CA

1.

To excel is to do better today
than you did yesterday.

Compare your performance today with
yesterday's results. If you improved or
advanced, you excelled. If you see
room for more improvement, you are
looking at tomorrow's opportunity to
excel.

2.

Excellence demands that
you do your best,
not that you be the best.

Being the best is not what excellence is about. Doing your best should be the focus. Even if you are involved in competition, your focus should still be on giving your best performance.

3.

Regarding the repeated performance of a task, excellence is *improvement* over past effort.

When you do a job over and over again, you should get better at it. Better can mean with fewer errors, in less time, at a lower cost, or with more desirable results.

4.

The peak of performance today
is the point of reference
for excellence tomorrow.

You never know what your best is
until you do it. What you do today
may be your best. It then becomes the
benchmark for tomorrow. With experience to support you, tomorrow you
try for a better best.

5.

Excellence is forward motion.

Consider where you are headed. If you are moving closer to where you want to be, you are excelling.

6.

Along the path of a planned project,
excellence is *progress*
toward completion.

If you are working on a project, you can measure excellence by checking your daily progress. If today you are closer to completion than you were yesterday and the work you did was your best performance, you have excelled.

```
7.

Excellence will not
leave a job unfinished.
```

Even if you decide to pursue a different course, you must bring closure to
what you started. Closure can simply
mean admission to yourself and ac-
knowledgement to others involved of
your abandonment of the endeavor.

8.

Your innate greatness is revealed
through excellence.

The seed of greatness was planted
inside you when you were born. Your
mind, soul, and talents work together
to cultivate your greatness. Making
the best use of these tools keeps them
sharp.

9.

A commitment to excellence prompts you to run a little harder in the face of opposition.

When your course leads down hill, forward motion comes easy. When the course is up hill, you are required to shift gears into the drive that will keep you moving forward. The uphill course tests your drive for excellence.

10.

Excellence is the push to close the gap between a better performance and your best performance.

Doing your best should always be your objective. But sometimes you just do not feel like making the extra effort. When you are committed to excellence, you find that special *oomph* at the times when complacency or indifference wants to take over.

11.

In the presence of obstacles,
perseverance is excellence.

Along any path of life or success you
choose, you will encounter obstacles.
They are there to teach you perseverance.

12.

Excellence is not elusive;
it is just misunderstood.

Think of excellence as a process instead of a destination. Look at it as a commitment that you make instead of a target that you hit. As a process or commitment, excellence will not elude you. It is immediately available and attainable.

13.

Excellence does not mean
to be without error.

The end result of what you do may
have mistakes or flaws. The excellence question is not whether it is
perfect but whether you improved or
advanced.

14.

Excellence does not strive
to be perfect but
to work without error.

Excellence would be an impossibility if
it required being perfect. No human
being is perfect. But with an attitude
of perfection, you can work toward the
goal of minimizing errors.

15.

Excellence is not the destination;
it is the way of getting there.

Can those who lie, cheat, or destroy others in order to reach their destination be considered to have excelled? Yes, if excellence is a destination. No, if excellence is the manner of getting there.

16.

Excellence is not
something you reach for;
it is the measure of your reach.

When you reach for a goal, excellence
is judged by how much you had to
stretch to get it. Excellence is in the
force of motion, not in the distance
covered.

17.

The goal does not matter;
the best way to get there
is through excellence.

The loftiness of your goal does not define your excellence. It is rather the state of your mind and the character of your heart which accompany your actions which demonstrate excellence.

18.

The moment you rise again,
you have excelled a failure.

Are you immune to failure? No, you
are not. If you fail, try again. Rising
again after a fall is upward motion.

19.

Greatness is your being;
excellence is your doing.

You were born in greatness. You are
a great being. Advancing, improving,
and performing your best, which are
the functions of excellence, are the
things you do to manifest the greatness
of your being.

20.

Excellence involves the body, mind, and soul.

Excellence can only come from total attention to the job. You can perform a task (body involvement) without thinking about it (mind involvement), but it may not be done right. If you do it without your heart (soul involvement), it will not be done well.

21.

If you are not enjoying
what you are doing,
you cannot excel at it.

Do you dislike your job? If so, you cannot and will not put your heart in it. If your heart is not in what you do, it is not your best.

22.

Where there is no meaning
in what you do,
there will likely be mediocrity
in your performance.

When you discover your unique purpose, it will be foremost in your thinking and feeling. If you cannot see or
feel purpose in what you do, you will
be mentally and spiritually detached
from it.

23.

The role of love in excellence
begins with loving yourself.

What's love got to do with it? Everything. Your desire for excellence is
based on love of yourself. If you did
not love yourself, the quality of what
you do would not matter to you. Nor
would it matter what others thought of
your work.

24.

You cannot love yourself and be satisfied with less than your best.

A commitment to excel is a promise you make to yourself. The person for whom you work is just a third-party beneficiary. You harm yourself when you break the commitment and put out mediocre work.

25.

Excellence cannot be managed from the outside; it must be directed from within.

Someone else can expect excellence from you and can monitor your work product, but no one can make you do your best. You alone control whether your performance will be excellent or mediocre.

26.

To excel is a personal commitment.

You must decide on excellence as your standard of performance. No one else can decide it for you. You must make a pact with yourself to stay on the course of excellence no matter what.

27.

Excellence begins the moment
you repudiate mediocrity
and resolve to excel.

There is no waiting period or special
benchmark to reach before you attain
excellence. It begins when you shake
off mediocrity and commit to moving
forward.

28.

Your commitment to excellence will be attacked by disappointment, discouragement, and despair.

A commitment to excellence is not easy to keep, especially when things do not go the way you want them to or the way you planned. Though you may feel down in spirit, do not be deterred from moving forward.

29.

In the wake of disappointment,
excellence responds with persistence.

When you are rejected, turned down,
or laid off, you will undoubtedly feel
disappointment. That is a normal
emotional reaction. Keep trying.
Keep moving forward. That is persistence.

30.

Money cannot buy a commitment
to excellence, but it may buy
a commitment to money.

You will commit to excellence or you
will not. Money is not a deciding
factor. If you work harder because
you are paid more money, it is out of
a sense of obligation to the money and
not a commitment to excellence.

31.

There is no challenge
that excellence is not willing to meet.

The two possible responses to a challenge are to surrender or to fight. You can never advance by giving up. A challenge forces your best performance by making you summons your reserve strength.

32.

Excellence welcomes change.

An environment where change is not occurring is a stagnant one. Stagnant surroundings do not invite or encourage development. Opportunities for growth are presented when there are changes in your living conditions and work environment.

33.

Excellence will always push you outside your comfort zone.

Have you reached the top of your game in that it takes you little effort to do the job well? If so, it is time for you to step across your line of proficiency into a new territory.

34.

Idleness stifles excellence.

It is obvious that if you are idle, you are not moving forward. To excel you must be moving, but do not confuse motion with progress. You can be in motion and yet not advance, as though on a treadmill.

35.

Organizational mediocrity
will stifle
individual excellence.

If you are on a ship whose engines are idle, you will drift along with the ship. If the ship doesn't advance, then you won't advance, no matter how hard you work on the deck. In relation to the ocean, your advancement is limited to that made by the vessel.

36.

An organization cannot excel
if its members
do not collectively excel.

The work of an organization is the combined efforts of its members. Hence, the organization's excellence cannot be judged by individual excellence but must be determined by the advancement or improvement of the group as a whole.

37.

One member's mediocrity
will diminish the potential
for excellence of the organization.

If your job is essential to the group,
your best performance is necessary for
the group's best performance. If you
content yourself with mediocrity, you
will negatively impact the group's
potential to advance.

38.

Outdo the competition and
you might excel.
Outdo yourself and you will.

The best measuring stick for excellence is always your own performance. It is possible for you to outdo the competition and still underperform yourself. And underperformance is not excellence.

39.

To win tells how you scored against the opposition; to excel tells how you played the game.

Winning and excelling both concern your performance but are based on different standards. In winning, your present performance is judged against your present opposition. In excelling, your present performance is compared with your past performance.

40.

The losers in life are those who languish in mediocrity.

You were born to win, to triumph, and to be great. By settling for mediocrity you give up your birthright.

41.

Team excellence fosters
individual excellence.

When individuals perform in a group,
they can provide for each other inspi-
ration and opportunity for top performance. The team must function at its
best to offer the best environment for
each member's performance.

42.

Competition within a team
will impede team excellence.

When an individual competes against
a team member, he or she is forced to
act in self-interest rather than in group
interest. Selfishness more often dimin-
ishes rather than enhances the efforts
of a group.

43.

Team excellence requires a
what's-in-it-for-*us* rather than
a what's-in-it-for-*me*
way of thinking.

For a group to do its best, each member must have the assurance that he will be supported and not undermined by his fellow team members. If one person takes the *for-me* approach, all will have to do the same for self-preservation.

44.

It is unfortunate, but sometimes mediocrity gets the award.

Awards are often given based on standards that do not measure excellence but rather the ability to hit a certain mark. Often there isn't even an identifiable mark. Politics and favoritism can play significant roles.

45.

You will never see your best
if you are always looking
at someone else.

You can get ideas or learn techniques
by studying the performance of someone else. But to see your potential
you must, at some point, take your
eyes off the other person and look at
yourself.

46.

The average person is average.

If you aspire to be like everyone else, you will probably succeed. It does not require a major commitment or much effort to be average.

47.

If your colleagues do a mediocre job,
you can do better than they
and still not excel.

Three factors determine best effort:
capabilities, circumstances, and intent.
Since all three of these are unique to
each individual, you cannot judge *your*
best effort by someone else's performance.

48.

Good enough is not good enough
for the person who seeks to excel.

"Good enough for what" is the question. Enough to warrant the pay
check? Enough to appease the boss?
Enough to maintain the status quo?
Such apathy or complacency does not
allow you to do your best.

49.

If there is no push for excellence,
the tendency will be
toward mediocrity.

Because excellence is forward motion,
it requires effort. No movement is
stagnation; to make progress, you must
take action. Your efforts and actions
are the forces that keep you from
resting in mediocrity.

50.

The measuring stick for excellence is your own performance, not the achievements of someone else.

You should not set the achievements of someone else as a benchmark for your excellence. To do so would make excellence a goal rather than a process.

51.

If you do not remember
where you came from, you will not
know if you have progressed.

From time to time you must assess
your progress. Knowing your starting
point is essential. Resetting the starting point for the next evaluation is
equally as important.

52.

Only through self-evaluation
can you be certain of the quality
of your performance.

You are the best person to assess
whether or not you have excelled.
Excellence is not only what you do but
the spirit in which you do it. Only you
know your intent and the extent to
which your heart was involved.

53.

Excellence is not just
a standard for working;
it is a way of living.

When you commit yourself to excellence, it is for life. That is to say, you commit to living your best, living to improve, and living to advance. Your commitment will be reflected in everything you do.

54.

If at first you do not succeed, it is an ideal opportunity to excel.

Your commitment to excellence is not a guarantee against failure. It is a guarantee that you will try again.

55.

Excellence is undaunted by
what seems to be unfair.

Many things that happen may seem to
you to be unfair. Some of them probably are. You should not compromise
your standards because someone else
has compromised theirs.

56.

Excellence is your best performance
toward the goal even if
the goal is not reached.

Sometimes goals are too lofty. Sometimes unanticipated problems arise. The fact that you did not reach your goal is not necessarily a negative reflection on your performance. Did you do your best?

57.

Money may induce you to show up,
but your desire for excellence
is what impels you
to give your best performance.

You are probably like most people;
they go to work to get money. But the
spirit in which you perform your job
emanates from an internal motivation.

58.

Excellence is its own reward.

It is gratifying to be rewarded for a job
well done. But the person committed
to excellence will do the job well without a reward.

59.

You cannot excel at what you do
if your sole inducement to perform
is outside your soul.

Giving your best is a soulful action.
Your soul does not get involved unless
it is touched. It cannot be touched by
things that are outside it, such as money and reward. It must be touched by
love or purpose.

60.

You may reach your goal,
but excellence requires that
your goal reach your heart.

Your achievements are of no value if
they do not satisfy your heart. Excellence thrives on that heartfelt satisfaction.

61.

Winning is synonymous
with excellence when you outdo
both your competitor and yourself.

Set for yourself a goal that surpasses
your past performance. Concentrate
on doing your best to reach that goal.
You will either win or lose. If you
lose, you will know that you could not
do anything about it because you did
your best.

62.

You can succeed without excelling, but you cannot excel without succeeding.

Achieving your goals does not necessarily require making your best effort. On the other hand, when you excel--advance or improve, you are successful.

63.

Quality of life is not measured
by the value of your things but is
judged by the quality of your living.

If you commit yourself to living in
excellence, you will ensure yourself
quality of life. It will not matter what
you own. Life is the result of living
not of owning.

64.

If the principles by which you live
are not governed by excellence,
they will have little value.

The rules that you live and work by--
such as honesty, integrity, fidelity,
respect--dictate what you will do in
given situations. Your commitment to
excellence determines how willing you
are to apply such principles. Frequent
application gives them value.

65.

Excellence will never promote self
to the detriment of another
individual.

Pushing another person down or pull-
ing someone back may give you the
sense that you are advancing. That is
neither the standard nor the spirit of
excellence.

66.

Excellence makes adjustments
where mediocrity makes excuses.

When you make excuses for your work,
you argue for the acceptance of mediocrity. By making the excuse, you
acknowledge that your performance
could have been better. Never will
there be a good argument for a mediocre performance.

67.

The boss can demand performance but cannot order excellence.

When you accept an offer of employment, you agree to perform certain duties in exchange for pay. Your superiors can require you to do specific tasks. But only you control the spirit in which you do them.

68.

Corporate excellence requires competent, comprehensive, and compassionate leadership.

A group leader must be able to touch the soul to inspire an individual to give his best. She then must direct each individual to the point where his best performance is in the best interest of the group. A heartless leader will develop a careless following.

69.

Excellence must include
a program for continuing education.

By increasing your knowledge you facilitate advancement, improvement, and top performance. You should always be in a learning mode. You can learn from your experiences as well as from formal training.

70.

Excellence seeks to
discover and develop
your hidden and unused talents.

You have been endowed with special
abilities to fulfil your purpose and live
in excellence. Discover your hidden
talents. Develop those that are unused. All your talents are essential to
getting the most out of life.

71.

If you do not excel,
you will stagnate or degenerate.

There are two alternatives to forward
motion--backward motion and idleness.
Moving backwards is degeneration; not
moving at all is stagnation. The direc-
tion of your actions is your choice.

72.

If you act just to be accepted, you will fall into the trap of mediocrity.

Are you doing what you do just to be accepted by others? The average person is average and is willing to accept you so long as you are similar. You can get what you want with a mediocre performance.

73.

The rat race is not run
on a track of excellence
but in a maze of mediocrity.

If you feel as though you are in a rat
race, you are probably competing for
things that do not matter. Excellence
is a track on which you can run and
you do not have to compete. You set
the pace.

74.

The opposite of excellence
is self-destruction.

Since excellence is forward motion, its
opposite is backward motion. If you
are moving backwards in personal
development, character, and performance, you are in a self-destructive
mode.

75.

Excellence will show itself
even when no one is looking.

Do you perform your job well only
when you are watched? How many
times have you let sloppy work go by
thinking that no one will ever know?
But *you* know. And whose opinion
about your performance is more important than yours?

76.

Those who excel are not driven;
they are leading.

Excellence is not the work of over-
achievers. It is the standard of living
chosen by those who want to enjoy the
fullness of life.

77.

The push for excellence
is sometimes painful.

You can get hurt by someone else
when the only thing that you have
done is the right thing. If you find a
way to soothe the pain you can keep
moving forward.

78.

Excellence makes mistakes
and learns from them.

You can advance or improve from the
mistakes that you make. If you allow
them to be a source for learning, you
transform them from error to education.

79.

The trap of mediocrity
is baited with comfort and security.

Being comfortable in one's position and feeling secure about one's job are two conditions that can lure you into mediocrity. You become content with an at-rest position. You stop moving forward.

80.

Excellence will survive
being overseen and can survive
being overlooked.

There is no reason for you to be uneasy about having your work scrutinized. Being committed to excellence, you do not have to alter your way of doing things. And you will keep doing it well even if your work is not recognized.

81.

The person who seeks to excel can find the opportunity to do so in any circumstance.

When you are committed to advancing, improving, and doing your best, your attention focuses on ways that you can make it happen. No matter how the circumstances change or what challenges the change brings, you look for the chance to excel.

82.

When you seek to excel,
you will find ways
around the obstacles to excellence.

Conditions which present obstacles
include poor funding, inadequate
equipment, mediocre support staff,
incompetent leadership, co-worker
jealousy, and dislike of your work.

83.

The commitment to excellence
requires daily renewal.

Your renewal may entail a simple
reminder of your commitment as you
face a trying situation. It could involve
a recreational diversion, a motivational
recharge, or a spiritual revival. You
must ascertain what you need to
strengthen your commitment.

84.

If today you are not challenged,
you will miss tomorrow's opportunity
to excel.

Challenges are like exercise for your
spirit. You can be strengthened by
them. When they push you to the
limit, you learn of the extent of your
capabilities.

85.

Progress can be tracked and quality can be rated, but the commitment to excellence is immeasurable.

Your capacity for excellence cannot be quantified, rated, or otherwise measured. It is as high as your ideals, as broad as your imagination, and as deep as your soul.

86.

Ability tempered with tenacity
and sharpened with excellence
is the competitive edge.

Two people of comparable skills will
obtain different results depending on
their willingness to persevere in the
endeavor and their commitment to
excel in the process.

87.

Excellence requires
spiritual replenishment to avoid
motivation depletion.

It is obvious to most people that the
body needs rest and the mind needs
diversion. To maintain excellence, the
spirit too requires revival. Otherwise,
the enthusiasm for excellence will die.

88.

The strength of your commitment to excellence is directly related to the worth you find in your work.

Do you see value in what you do? If not, you will likely not care about how you do the job. The more value you place in what you do, the more committed you will be to doing it well.

89.

Raw talent is refined
through excellence.

You cannot just practice, practice, practice to develop your talent. You must practice well, practice well, practice well. If you practice mediocrity, you will become quite adept at mediocrity.

90.

Quality can be controlled and
time can be managed,
but people must be loved.

Management and control does not
cultivate or promote excellence. To
promote the spirit that sparks excellence, you must touch the soul of an
individual, and the soul is touched only
by love.

91.

People who place value in themselves
rather than in their jobs
are easily committed to excellence.

You are valuable. Your worth is in
your being. The quality of what you
do reflects your perception of your
own worth. When you perceive yourself to be valuable, you readily trans-
mit value to what you do.

92.

A depraved heart cannot fulfill a commitment to excellence.

A heart that is absent love and filled with malice or ill-will has intentions that work toward destruction. This is the opposite of the intentions of excellence--advancement and improvement.

93.

The person with a closed mind will eventually run into the wall created by his or her limited thinking.

The mind for excellence must be open to allow room for new ideas and a free movement of imagination. When the mind is closed, it forms a limited field of ideas and approaches.

94.

You can plow through the field
of uncertainty as long as you believe
in the possibilities.

Excellence requires your willingness to
extend yourself into new areas. There
will always be uncertainty in such
stretching. Believing in the possibilities gives you confidence to stretch.

95.

The realm of possibilities and
the field of uncertainty occupy
the same space; their difference is
in how you approach them.

There is a degree of uncertainty in
everything that you do. There is the
possibility of success in everything that
you attempt. You decide whether you
will cower to the uncertainty or charge
toward the possibilities.

96.

In order to do your best, you must be able to discern when to move up and when to move on.

The move that will lead you to excel and perform your best is the one that will give you joy, that will make you stretch, that will stimulate your thinking and creativity, and that will utilize your talents.

97.

If what you do is governed
by what you own, the quantity of
your possessions will take priority
over the quality of your performance.

If you are working at a job that you
dislike because you need the money to
pay for what you own, your possessions
are in control. You are sacrificing
your greatness for your goods.

98.

Time spent on relaxation, recreation,
and reflection is rejuvenation
not stagnation of excellence.

Idleness will lead to mediocrity. However, stopping to rest, to relax, and to
recreate, is not idleness.   A recess
from work and the day-to-day drudger-
ies of life is necessary for the rejuvenation of your spirit.

99.

The fullness of life is not measured
by the length of time
or the breadth of experience
but by the height of spirit.

Living a long life is desirable. Achieving much success is laudable. But the
fullness of your life will be judged by
the spirit in which you lived and did
what you did.

100.

Life is not a contest or game
or race to the finish line.

Life is more akin to an exercise. You
rise, stretch, push, or run to excel. It
should be done not to compete against
someone else but to develop your
greatness.

101.

Everyone can excel.

Many things operate on the scarcity principle. One team wins. Limited positions available. Grading on a curve. There is, however, no limit of opportunity for excellence. The only scarcity that may exist is in the number of those who will seek it.

102.

Now is the best time to commit to excellence because *then* is gone and *when* may not come.

It does not matter what has happened in the past; you can't do anything about it. It does not matter what will happen in the future; you do not know how much of it you will see. What matters is now.

103.

Excellence encourages
the excellence of others.

Your life is inextricably intertwined
with the lives of the people around
you--your family, friends, colleagues.
In effect, you are on the same life
team with them. You advance when
you encourage their advancement.

104.

Planted in the soul of each individual
is the seed of greatness.

When all is said and done, the question will be: *Did you cultivate and develop your greatness?*

ACKNOWLEDGMENTS

I am grateful to my wife, Jacqueline J. LaMon, for her willingness to read, reread, and read again the manuscript. Her editorial suggestions and her proofreading skill ensured that the content and appearance of this book reflected its title.

I thank Kevin Coffee for his editorial contribution to this book. I sought his input because I was sure that he knew excellence.

As the manuscript came off the printer, Linnea, my eight-year-old daughter, read each principle. The excitement in her voice as she read assured me of the value of the project. Thank you Linnea.

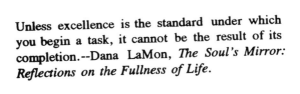

Unless excellence is the standard under which you begin a task, it cannot be the result of its completion.--Dana LaMon, *The Soul's Mirror: Reflections on the Fullness of Life*.

About the Author

Dana LaMon is a world champion motivational speaker. He earned the distinction of World Champion in 1992 from Toastmasters International. In 1993 Toastmasters awarded him the Accredited Speaker designation.

Now forty-seven years old, Dana has been blind since age four. Despite this visual disadvantage, he earned a bachelor of arts degree in mathematics from Yale University and a law degree from the University of Southern California. He has been a member of the California State Bar since 1978. In 1981 he began serving as an Administrative Law Judge.

Since 1991 Dana LaMon has provided motivational keynotes and seminars to help people around the world seek excellence and develop greatness. He speaks to audiences from corporate executives to kindergarten students; from religious congregations to prison inmates. He has delivered his message to audiences from Honolulu, Hawaii, to Johannesburg, South Africa.

Other books by Dana LaMon:

THE SOUL'S MIRROR:
Reflections on the Fullness of Life

MASTER THE CEREMONIES:
The Emcee's Handbook of Excellence

For more information about the author, his
speaking availability, his books, his audio and
video tapes, you can contact ImageWorth at:

Post Office Box 6108
Lancaster, CA 93539
Tel: (661) 949-7423
Fax: (661) 942-7478
E-mail: dana@danalamon.com
www.danalamon.com